BAND NERDS
Confessions & Confusion

Quotes from **The 13th Chair** Trombone Player

Written By
DJ Corchin

Illustrated By
Dan Dougherty

The phazelFOZ Company, LLC

Published by The phazelFOZ Company, LLC.
Chicago, Illinois
www.phazelfoz.com

Library of Congress Number 2014953132

ISBN   9780996078153 (Hardcover)
         9780996078146 (Paperback)
         9780996078160 (eBook)

The
13th
Chair

All quotes are original. Any resemblance to other quotes is strictly coincidental. Those other quotes are probably the lame version of these though.

Part of The 13th Chair's

BAND NERDS

Book Series

Belief

So often we look at someone who is fighting for music education as a passionate individual. One who thinks if their voice is loud enough, it warrants an ear to listen. They see music education as a cause to be fought for, fists raised ready for battle. But what they really are is someone who has a strong belief that the implementation of music education is not only necessary but inevitable. Their fighting is simply the result of losing their patience with those who can't see the future as clearly...or as warmly. As music education advocates, we need to see ourselves as not just passionate individuals, but as people who have foresight into what is going to happen. We may learn to not lose our patience as quickly and instead of continuing to fight, we will begin to educate. Belief is something that can't be outshouted, outspent, or exhausted. It is simply a permanent result of what we all know to be true; When music is part of our education, the world is safer and its people richer.

**Dedicated to the music teachers
who always believe.**

I often think about what my life would be like if I played a different instrument. But I also think about if I was a crime fighting super hero who could turn invisible so that's not saying much.

Whenever we want to improve something we add music to it. A movie, we add music. Dining experience we add music. A sports event, music. Political gathering, music. But when it comes to our education system we take music away to improve it? I call shenanigans.

Life is dynamic, keep playing.

Funny we say, "You missed that note" instead of "Those 2457 notes were awesome!"

If that piece of music didn't move you, you must be dead. If you're dead, that explains the smell.

Some days I wish I could just hide from the world and crawl up in my instrument. Then I think about how gross that would be and suddenly the world doesn't seem so bad.

My instrument is part of me.
Literally there are bits of me inside it.

Sometimes I put a French horn mouthpiece on my finger and pretend I have an evil witch finger.

I'm gonna play the snot out of this piece you said
was too hard for me. And that will be enough for my
revenge. Well, I might pee on your house too.

They say to legitimize music as a real subject you have
to be able to test it, apparently through multiple choice
word questions.

Sometimes I close my eyes to get into the music, then I
lose my place.

Woodwinds have so many holes in them. I don't like my
instruments how I like my cheese.

Play your instrument for a baby. You'll enrich their life
and feel great knowing you can play better than them.

Let's spend 6 to 8 weeks working tirelessly to make
difficult parts more comfortable, make our air control
more comfortable, make our mallet and stick control
more comfortable, make posture and harmonizing
more comfortable, make our team's work ethic more
comfortable, then when it's time to showcase what
we've learned, let's put on awkward fitting, outdated
tuxes, itchy, heavy, too-long dresses, and sit in either a
sweaty, poorly lit gym or a too-small stage with lights
that double as the faculty microwave... and make some
beautiful fine artistic music.

It's socially awkward to NOT bring your oboe to a party.
Geesh.

Using words to describe music is saying crescendo just means to get louder.

I can't tell you how much I LOVE my instrument. You would be really jealous and slightly disturbed.

"We are what we repeatedly do. Therefore I am a conversation where I lie about practicing."

- Band Aristotle

I'm not giving you "the eyes" from across the band because I like you. We just rehearsed 10 measures for an hour because SOMEBODY didn't practice.

After graduation, I probably won't remember those meaningful times with my friends during that math test, the team building exercises in home ec., the emotional reactions to the chemistry experiments, the personal growth I had in physics, or the physical triumph of dodgeball day in gym class. But I will remember all that I did with my music family and who I became because of them (ok maybe dodgeball day also).

Sometimes you want to practice late at night. You don't, but you want to.

I like to think of ways that all the instruments can fit together to make a giant robot.

Sometimes in music you gotta break it down to build it up. Same goes for you.

Someone designed the sax with a bent neck because they were so laid-back they wanted the mouthpiece to come to them...and that's how jazz was born.

I know there's a lot of similarities between music and math but it's hard to get excited about that.

Didn't need to do cardio at the gym today. Got my heart worked out while practicing.

I can't imagine my life without music. Ok, I can imagine it, but it suuuuuuuucks.

Treat them like students and they'll listen.
Treat them like people and they'll find pride.
Treat them like leaders, they'll lead.
Treat them like musicians
and they'll find the music inside.

Sometimes it's easy to get musical phrases & breads mixed up. Like, "I'll have a roast beef sandwich on an olive sonata."

Sometimes life gives you an accidental.

**A bad rehearsal is still a step in the right direction.
It's just that step happened to be in dog poop.**

When you read a book, you experience the story restricted by words. When you watch a play or a dance, you're limited to only what is created for you. But when you listen to music, you can close your eyes and be a unicorn pterodactyl on a quest to save the land of Zangor from the evil Gorilla King, Keith.

A plain note with the right amount of air behind it
becomes a meaningful tone. Similar to how a booger
becomes a snot rocket.

If all you give is standardized tests, then all you get is
standardized people.

Music is about relationships and emotions so be careful
what you practice.

When I need to close my eyes and go to my happy place,
it tends to look like my band room.

"Wait, mom I think this present is for you."
"No it's for you."
"But it's two tickets to a show for you and Dad."
"Remember when we got you your instrument last year?"
"Yes."
"This year we got you time by yourself to practice."

Sometimes your director forgets to cue you in and
you're like "What the heck? I thought we had a deal?"

I might get lost in my music,
but I'm never lost with my music.

Want a good indicator as to how organized you'll be later in life? Look at your instrument locker. It's about as accurate as it gets.

Don't get mad at the person who no one told not to clap in-between movements. We were all that person at one point. Well everyone but me of course.

I don't believe that the music was already there, all I had to do was find it. I created my music therefore I am ruler of it. And I shall be called Your Royal Highness.

It's not just Thanksgiving, I always think of turkey, stuffing, and mash potatoes during rehearsal. It's my motivation.

Music is like a box of chocolates. You don't decide between the different types, you eat it all & worry about the consequences later.

"Excuse me. Do you have a pass?"
"I'm going to the band room."
"Oh. Ok then."

The applause at the end of your show is like a giant band hug. There's always that one person who goes a little too long and makes it awkward.

Sometimes I hear someone play something I connect with and I want to respond, "I know right?!"

Your eyes are the most beautiful whole notes I've ever seen. And I've seen A LOT of whole notes.

Do you practice with a sense of fear of what will happen
if you don't, or a sense of wonderment of would could
happen if you?

> Music makes me dance.
> Dancing makes me healthy.
> Healthy makes me happy.
> Happy makes me music.
> Don't ask questions, it just works.

Band people are the only people to cut class only to go
to another class.

> When they need it, I'll put the band on my
> shoulders and carry them through. They would
> do the same for me.

When you watch other bands perform remember
our similarities bring us together but our
differences make us stronger.

> Don't judge the band until you've marched a
> show in their shoes.

Be kind to the person volunteering to work the parking
lot. The band world is small. They're most likely the
parent of the person you're gonna marry.

Why do band directors use batons? Lame. I say the next time the director gets up on the podium they need to reach up behind their backs and pull out a barbarian sword. Conduct with THAT and see the emotion pour out of the band.

You might have the fancy expensive instrument but that just means it will hurt emotionally also when I hit you with it.

Instruments don't just amplify sounds, they amplify the heart.

Love your band and it will love you back.
Just sometimes not as gently.

No way I'm kissing you, I've seen your mouthpiece.

There is another entrance to Narnia located in the instrument storage room. Locker 19. But don't go through locker 20, that takes you to Mordor. Their music program is terrible.

It's ok if I lose my place in the music. The dude next to me that wants my chair is probably paying attention.

To me music is life. You should get a music.

Music means you're never alone.

Harmony doesn't mean you play the same notes. That's why it's beautiful.

**Conducting should be graceful, not like you're
shaking angrily. Unless you mean to shake angrily.
Then you need a hug.**

When you hold an instrument in your hand, suddenly
you're even more good looking. Not sure how it works but
it's essentially the equivalent effect of killer abs.

> People who don't understand why you would trust a
> fellow band member with your life have never done a
> pass through at 208 BPM.

Music can help you find yourself and lose your mind at
the same time.

> I DO work out. It's called the practice
> sweats thank you very much.

Lying in a private lesson about practicing isn't the bad
type of lying. It's more like not telling someone they're
ugly because you don't want to hurt their feelings.

> If the music lives inside me, I would like it to start
> paying rent. I have college to pay for.

When lots of the same instrument play together it can sound
pretty good, but when different instruments play together the
music is truly magical. When will the world figure that one out?

> I played the French horn once and felt
> awkward like when I jam my hand in there I
> might pull out a baby French horn.

The sousaphone is the hermit crab of the band.

Just for fun, sometimes I'll give someone across the band the death stare during the entire rehearsal, and then when it's over and they ask what's wrong I say, "Nothing, what do you mean? Let's sit together at lunch."

It's ok if your life is out of tune sometimes, just as long as you hear it.

If you miss a rehearsal you break a promise. If you break a promise you lose my trust. If we have no trust it's hard to love. Without love there's no music.

If you don't get why soft and slow is harder to play than loud and fast, then it's probably safe to say you need to work on your kissing as well.

Live life like you read music. A few measures ahead but always focused on what you're playing.

If music makes the world go round then all that stuff about gravitational forces and mathematical rotational equations was a waste of time.

The French horn is just as complicated as the people who play it.

Funny how people think drum major auditions are a one time thing at the end of the year.

**If I had a belt of piccolos I'd throw them like ninja
stars. Then wonder why I had a belt of piccolos.**

I'm pretty sure music doesn't care what color someone is, whether they like girls or boys or both, whether they believe in something or someone, how much money they have or want, or how many friends or followers they have. We should all be more like music.

Wouldn't it be great if music wasn't something you had to pay for, but rather something you could pay with?

I know music and math are closely related, but I like the music side of the family more. Why would you hang out with the "math" uncle?

If your instrument is smelly, you might be too. Better double check...no seriously, check.

If you do music right, it will never be perfect. Just beautiful and interesting...as the best things always are.

What if instruments were part of genetics? Like, you have the recessive bassoon gene. Would explain why there aren't that many. Yeah that explains it.

Just like music, when you lose your place, listen around you and pick it back up.

Heading to the gym. Gonna do some ear training.

"Why don't you play some holiday songs for us on
your clarinet?"
"No Grandma."
"Come on. It will be nice for the family."
"No it won't."
"Why not?"
"I play Euphonium."
"What the sam hell is a Euphiniumumm?"
"I love you Grandma."

Band is like social media. No matter
what your privacy settings are, everyone
still seems to see your every move.

Brass have an octave key too. It's just not very nice to
put your finger there.

Your band is like a baby. Sometimes they cry,
sometimes they laugh, sometimes they poop.
But you always love them.

Whether you're city, suburbs, or country we all
worry about the B major scale. So don't tell me we
can't find common ground.

I overheard an oboe and violin arguing over who could
play louder. I left the room as I had better things to do.

**Thor has his hammer.
I have my music.
We both bring the thunder.**

The only time I eat nachos, pretzels, and skittles
as a meal is at a marching band competition...and
sometimes on Tuesdays.

Sometimes the only way out of life's repeat is to
write your own music.

I once gave flowers to my drum major to tell her I loved her.
She ate them and made me use the stems to mark my spot.

I've worked out my instrument so much lately it's
grown pecs...and oddly enough, nipples.

Band is my core class. I take Algebra as an elective.
Gotta be well rounded.

Band nicknames are always a little naughtier
than regular ones.

The friendships you make in music will last the rest
of your life...or until chair placement auditions.
Whichever comes first.

When I haven't practiced my instrument in a while
and find myself staring at it, I swear it's staring back.

The mellophone is not the most laid back instrument.
Kind of like Iceland doesn't really have ice.

My instrument gives me warm fuzzies inside. Only when I don't clean it out for a while though.

The funny thing is, people who make jokes about
band camp really don't know the half of it. So really
we're laughing AT you.

They say playing music for a baby while it's still in
the womb is great for its development. So I took a
trumpet out and blew her little undeveloped face off.

That's not a glow, it's sweat. You don't play the best
show of your life with glow.

I will make you love me. You are my instrument.
You will love me, I will play you, and you will like it.

If everyone was the same, the world would be like a
symphony with only one kind of note. Who wants to
listen to that?

Be a section leader not a section manager.

The only appropriate time to fart in rehearsal is
before the first breath of the downbeat. That way
everyone tastes it.

One of these days in that moment when my director
makes eye contact with me right before my solo, I'm
going to look back like, "What? Me?"

**If you have to get me clothes for my birthday,
the only acceptable item is a marching
uniform that goes on like Iron Man.**

Wait, you want me to balance AND blend?
I can't work like this.

Shhh I'm practicing long tones...in my head.

With my ears plugged I opened my eyes, but still felt
like I couldn't see. With my eyes closed, I unplugged
my ears and never saw more clearly.

Some saxes play to the side, some play in the
center. What is that, like different forms of
karate or something?

Why do piccolos split into two pieces to fit in a case?
I think it's just to patronize the larger instruments.

I'm sorry, I try, but I can't look at the bassoon and not
think..."Whaaat?...How...How did someone think of
this thing?"

It doesn't matter how much you try to hurt me, it will
never hurt as bad as getting my hand pinched in my slide.

Usually we meet our heroes and they aren't what we
expected them to be. Sometimes we see our directors and
they aren't we thought they'd be. That doesn't mean heroes
aren't heroic, or directors can't be inspirational. It just
means they're imperfect...like they're supposed to be.

Weird how some people have no problem
practicing their conducting in public with their
headphones on, but when it comes to dancing,
no no that's too embarrassing.

Marching band is supposed to stimulate the senses. Just
not your sense of smell.

> The director looks down at the boy & asks what
> do u want to play? The boy smiles & plainly says,
> euphonium. Silence ensues. Both are confused.

True friendship is when you share a look across the band
after your director says something really dumb and its
exactly what you texted about the night before... verbatim.

> Sometimes I feel out of my comfort zone like when I
> learn a new scale. But if I keep practicing suddenly life
> gets a little easier and I might even start to prefer sharps.

I never touch the pound symbol on my phone. It looks
sharp. B'dump ching Heeeyoooo!

> Yeah I went surfing today...on the waves of
> perfectly locked 5ths. Oh snap!

If I could cast one music spell it would be for one good entrance.
Just one! ... that magically makes me have 5 million dollars,
chiseled abs, speak French, a moderately decent car like an Audi,
make healthy stuff taste like twinkies, use the force anytime I
want, can become invisible (with my clothes on, and not a special
suit, MY OWN CLOTHES) a dog that doesn't poop, invent the
fold-up trombone with cup holder, an adult-size big wheel WITH
FLAME DECALS ...oh and world peace. Damn, I always forget
world peace.

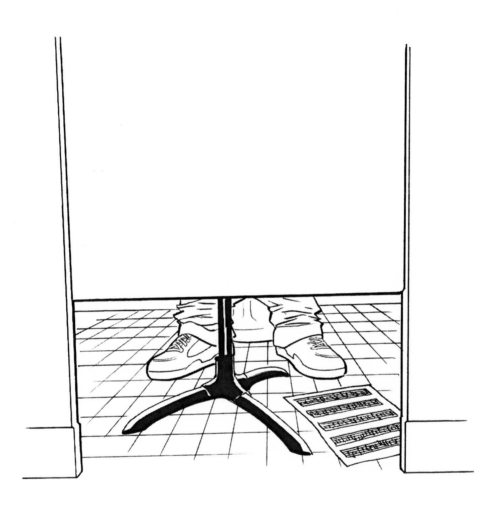

There should be music stands in all bathrooms. That way you never have to stop the joy of practicing.

When I say I love this piece I mean I have a solo in it.

Since you're across the band and we can't hold
hands, I will move my eyebrows up and down during
measures 45-55. That's how you'll know I love you.

We empty our spit on the ground but in our minds,
instantly it evaporates. Magic is amazing

My instrument is like a hot dog. I don't know
what's in it, but I keep putting it in my mouth.

When someone says, "You need to stop and smell the
roses" I usually reply, "I can't. I'll be in a practice room all
day and when I stop, it definitely won't smell like roses."

Music should have just the right amount of
silliness in it.

Music is always evolving. Musicians should too.

I may not be able to sightread, but I can lip read from
across the band.

Sometimes I think about music while I'm playing other
music.

I secretly have a crush on you from across the band and really appreciate the 15 measures the composer wrote where we both rest. It gives me time to try and lock eyes with you "accidentally."

A politician threatening a teacher's job in order to get better test scores is like an engineer telling you you'll be kicked out of band if you don't play more right notes.

If I could paint like Van Gogh I would practice my music more. Ya know, because I can already paint like Van Gogh.

If you're gonna march to the beat of your own drum, better make sure you practice more than the other drums.

Great french horn players are like Olympic archers just with pitch...and deadly accurate sass.

Don't tell musicians there is math in how music is made. It's like telling them there's vegetables in the food they like.

I don't know about you but for some reason I feel more in shape with shoulder pads and gauntlets.

I don't need a therapist. Just my instrument...and maybe some skittles.

Music is a time machine in so many ways.

**You're not serious about music unless you tattoo
it to your face.**

Play their part before you judge.

Sometimes you sound pretty bad. Then I think about all the hard work, the hours of practice, the hundreds and thousands of dollars that went into it. Yeah, that should really sound better.

"I'm going to my locker."
"But that's the band room."
"Mind your business."

Band people seem to be at peace with their spit.

There's a reason we're called a "band." We're in it together, we're all connected, and we wrap around open bags of chips so they don't go stale.

When your director makes the group repeat over and over again the 10 measures before the solo you've been practicing and then ends rehearsal, it's like waiting in line at Disney World for hours only to be told it's closed when you get to the front. Noooooo!

If I sweat during my first week of concert band it's not because I'm out of shape, I'm just reminiscing about marching season.

If the music moves you, you can ease up on the fiber.

You can pick your friends. You can pick
your nose. You can pick your friend's nose.
Just not during rehearsal. Save that for the
concert. Then give it everything you got.

Marching band audience cheers are always more
rhythmically accurate than "normies."

> If I won an award it's because I happened to. If I
> won the audience's heart it's because I meant to.

Next time you're bored, try staring at someone very
seriously and don't say a word no matter what. Then
after they get fed up with you not answering them grab
your instrument and play a major scale in thirds, look at
them again and walk away mad. It helps pass the time.

> In the moments before the performance,
> I look for laughter.

Music is plucking the right sounds from the right
emotions. Like a perfect eyebrow. Pluck. Pluck. Pluck.

> You have mastered your marching technique when
> people with a trained eye can't tell you have to pee.

Band people are extremely innovative. Just yesterday I
used my spit valve to untie my shoe.

> If you march in the same band or corps you're officially
> related. Like 6th cousin three times removed or someth'n.
> Changes your perspective on relationships don't it?

You must be quarter note triplets. 'Cause when I'm with you it seems like time is slowing down.

My doctor told me he played in orchestra & band in high school. I suddenly felt much better. Then he took out the rubber gloves.

Sometimes I don't need an inspirational speech or motivational team building exercise. Sometimes I just need to BE with my music family.

I can't come to your concert. I have that thing...you know...when I listen to you play, I get diarrhea.

No matter how hard you try, your reed will never smell as good as it did out of the box.

Sometimes late at night I wish I was a string player. One with long hair that can fly everywhere when I play forte on a killer concerto while my bow is shredding and catching on fire. Then I would hold it up while it was being engulfed by flames and yell, "I HAVE THE POWER!"

I believe music education is a right.

You'd think we'd see more vampire musicians. They live forever so you'd figure at some point they'd say, "Hey I've always wanted to learn the saxophone."

I'm not tone deaf. I'm just ignoring them.

I want to tape conducting batons to all of my
fingers and then eat a lot of olives.

Ok I get the science behind it, but I still think it's
weird sometimes there are holes in the keys that
cover other holes on flutes.

Bass trombone players don't play trombone,
they play BASS trombone.

You think, "Trumpet, that will be easy. It's only got
3 valves." Then you learn about the left hand tuning
slide and you're like, "What the hell is this?"

We should pronounce "flute" with two syllables
as in "fa-lutes, fa-lutes, fa-lutes are on fire!"

Every euphonium player EVERY TIME has
a moment right after they tell someone what
instrument they play of "am I going to have to
explain this?"

There's something to be said for being last chair. You get
the best perspective when everything else is in front of you.

The music speaks to me. Usually it's pretty inappropriate.

You're always just a half step away from changing
the quality and feel of your relationship.

Why don't we have trees in band rooms? They produce oxygen which encourages better breathing and we can have monkeys.

When someone asks, "Hey nerd, why a feather in your marching hat" I say "It's not a feather, it's a polycarbonate synthetic resin...dork."

Sometimes I have dirty band thoughts like playing an F# in the key of Ab just to be bad. Makes me feel naughty.

Music is like chicken pox. Once you catch it, it's always in your body and it's better to get it when you're young.

My morning coffee is a session of long tones and a nice étude. Followed by a cup of coffee.

Don't let your mouth get in the way of your music.

I'm not squinting because of the sun. I have laser beam focus and I'm not afraid to use it. I'm talking to you, judges.

"You have mud on your shoes."
"I know, it was a great show!"
"We were in a dome."
"I really like marching band."

I even 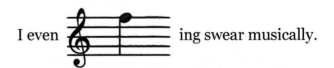 ing swear musically.

I laugh at those cartoons that have a musician
playing so loud their tongue comes out of the bell.
But then think, wait that would be really gross.

There's a fine line between humor and sarcasm. It's
usually right between the low brass and French horns.

People will think twice to mess with
me if I poop in their bell.

When your own mouthpiece grosses you
out, it's time to finally clean it.

Sometimes I feel like the whole world's my band room.
Then I realize the world has a long way to go.

If I have to clap and count, you have to conduct
and do math. Hard math. Carry the one with a
remainder type math.

I use my slide spray bottle sometimes to shoo away pests
and percussionists. I recommend one for all instruments.

Playing concert snare after winter drumline
practice has got to be like performing surgery
after a few energy drinks.

In the future, music will be in 3D.

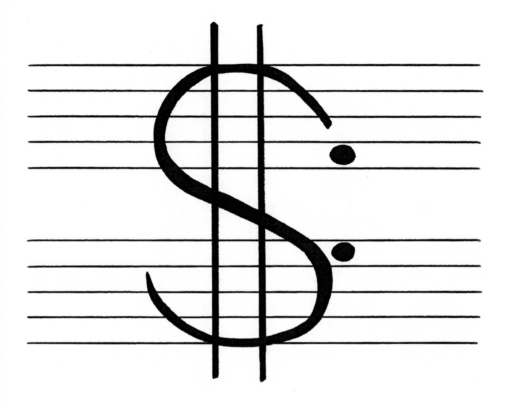

A unifying clef for today's musical cynic.

I like that breathing, the thing that gives me life, gives
me music. Guess that's true for mom also. Instrument
rentals were expensive.

Band makes me sweat in all the wrong places.

All chair challenges should be to the death. That way
when rehearsals start everyone gets a solo.

Make sure saying "I Promise" doesn't
become your "One more time."

I challenge you world, to not let your music
humor be cliché and dumb.

Not sure which is worse, brass mouth,
reed taste, or percussion breath.

If you're in music then you have ninja hearing and
can probably do one roundhouse kick.

I marinate my rare steak with valve oil. Aarrggg!

Oh oboe player, just let it all out.
Let out all the air, you will feel better.

Admit it, you have mastered the art of moving your hand
like you're marking your part but don't have a pencil, even
scraping your nail slightly to give that unique writing sound.

Just listen to me play and you'll understand.

In everything you do, somehow, someway, make it special.

I like to make robotic sound effects when
assembling my instrument.

No, I didn't miss a note. It's my way of breaking up with you.

What if the reed stayed still and the
instrument vibrated? Whoa.

Practicing is a great alternative to crying about it.

"I just need more time with you. You're always at
rehearsal or practicing."
"It makes me happy. You don't want me happy?"
"Wait, is that a trick question?"
"No. I'm pretty sure you want me to be happy and not
angry to the point where I slash your tires."
"Yes then. You're sounding really good at that fast
part that seems really difficult."
"Thank you! I've been working really hard at it."

**You can take a bath with a brass instrument to clean it.
Advantage Brass.
(Don't take a bath with your instrument.)**

I'm not just emptying my spit valve,
I'm dispelling the demons.

> When we're a beginner, the 6am rehearsals
> somehow weren't a big deal...and now...I don't
> wanna talk about it...need coffee.

I fell out of step because I just wanted a little attention.

> I accidentally breathed in through my
> instrument and now I feel kinda funny.

Take a moment to laugh. It's meant to have its
own moment. Otherwise you'd be able to do it
while playing your instrument.

> I feel too much pressure when someone
> asks me what my favorite type of music is.

I got into music education because of the money.

> Someone write a piece of music that incorporates
> random sounds of bubble wrap. Watch practicing
> increase 10 fold. No one can resist the hypnotic
> urge to pop.

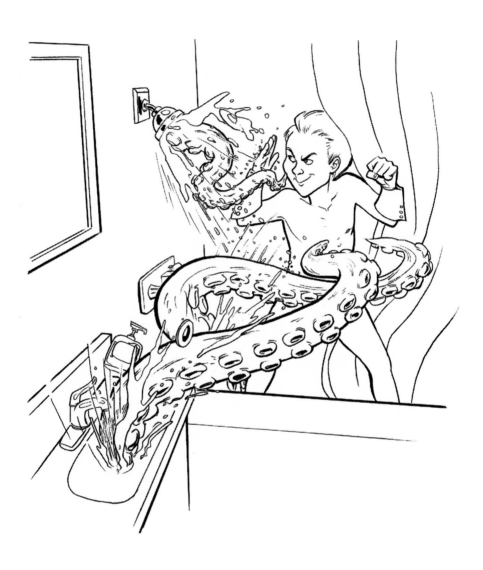

As long as you keep your gauntlets on, you have super powers. Never take them off. Not even in the shower. You never know what evil lurks in the shower.

Music makes the world go round...then we get dizzy, fall down, and throw up.

Got it. Conductor podium that's a treadmill. No more excuses Director.

When you ask another band nerd on a date, just remember playing etudes for each other is NOT romantic. Unless, "playing etudes" is a metaphor, then...well...

Music is a place to go when you feel like there's nowhere else.

Do flute players fart with vibrato too? Geeze.

Carpet in the band room itself is not necessarily a terrible idea, but when it starts to get squishy is when I get concerned.

I wish I had a harness where I could wear my trombone on my back & take it out like a big battle ax.

Life should be a crescendo.

I'm so band I hula hoop with a sousaphone.

I love music so much I can't have it on in the background. I know you know what I mean.

When you leave the band room for the last time it will never be the same, but it will always be there.

Euphoniums should be called mephoniums. 'Cause it's all about me.

Admit it. You've done it too. Smelled the inside of your mouthpiece and was puzzled by the experience.

"You're 20 cents sharp."
"I have to poop."
"Oh."

I like to practice outside. But then I realize people can hear me so I only practice stuff I already play really well.

Anyone who tells you "it's just condensation" ask them to wipe it up with their hand and then lick their fingers. See what they say then.

Sometimes I take out my instrument not to practice, just to look in the mirror and see what I look like playing.

I heard a low note but the tuba player wasn't playing, just deviously grinning.

Sometimes I watch you play, stare intensely at your face and think... man I didn't know nostrils could move that way.

I wish I always had a stand with me so when I need to hide behind it, it's always there.

If I don't have my instrument I feel naked. That's the real reason I practice. I don't work out.

Sometimes I memorize my music on accident, but when I need to on purpose, I can't remember a thing.

The best player that wants to play 3rd or 4th part to learn and so others can play 1st is the section leader in my book.

I don't think you understand this relationship. You can touch me, not my instrument.

Music puts the epic in movies, the larger in life, and the touching in moments. Usually too much touching.

I hate when life gets in the way. Except when music is my life. Then I don't mind.

Some people's music comes from their heart. Mine comes from my left knee.

I watch myself practicing in a mirror to practice my sexy playing face. You know, in case I need it.

The shape of an English horn looks like if you blow hard enough it will give birth to a baby English horn.

Every time a school board wants to cut a music program, they should be required to play an instrument in that program for one month prior. We'll even give them an instrument locker and let them skip hot cross buns.

The world is like music. The more you experience the more you realize how much you didn't know.

Music is special. Like the not quite cooked all the way through but tastes like sugar wrapped in dreams made from love, cafeteria chocolate chip cookies special.

When you're not afraid to be humbled by the music you're playing, you're growing.

Music listens back. It just doesn't judge us in return. That's why we love it.

Can I put a repeat sign around you?

We're the same chord just a different inversion.

You have yoga, I have marching band.

**What if sections were actually alien races? Do you
think their spaceships would be shaped like their
instruments? That would be awesome.**

When I march backwards I have buns of steel. Pow!

Totally want to make music with you...no wait, out with you...no I was right, music with you.

Band peeps might high five awkwardly, but a tight sax soli usually offsets the ramifications.

When I cry, my tears fall in rhythm. Then I remix it.

What if practicing was caffeinated? I know I'd do it more.

The first time you see your director in shorts you're like, "Whoa, weird."

Band moms are not like regular moms. They may not have capes, but they can definitely shoot laser beams from their eyes. To not respect this will be your demise.

Sometimes when I'm alone in the band room, I'll stand on the podium, put my hands up like I'm gonna conduct, then think, "Huh, so this is what it looks like from up here." Then someone comes in and I act like I'm fixing the stand.

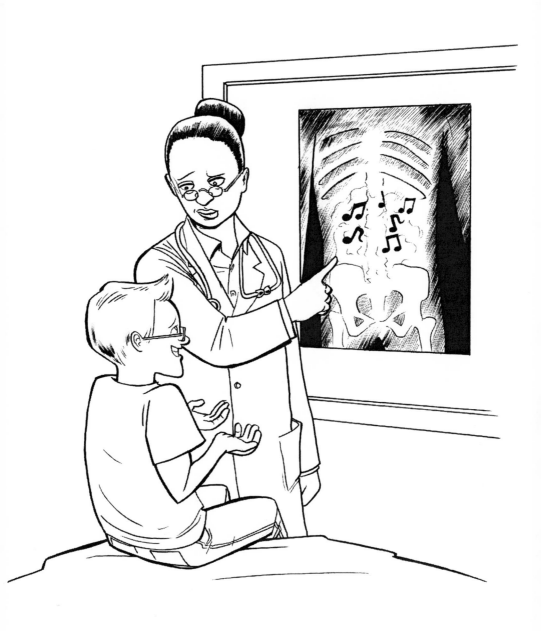

Music gets deep down in ya.
Like small intestines in ya.

OMG gravy makes everything better. I'm going to pour gravy all over my music.

> Marching band is something that is not bound by race, religion, economics, or geography. It is an activity that only unites us!

I would like to request we get to wear capes in rehearsal that are decorated based upon our individuality. For concerts, we'll compromise and put on our formal capes.

> I'd hug you but my uniform's too small and I can't lift my arms.

Instead of starting wars, let's start bands.

> The music world is so small I'm pretty sure you're my mother.

I hope my child has perfect pitch...and shapeshifting and teleporting powers.

> Funny how a poet and a musician can mean the same thing. And it's beautiful when they do.

It's my sectional. I'll pout if I want to.

Sometimes I'll hold my instrument case with a slightly bent arm while walking. It makes me look more muscular…ish.

Sometimes when we're having a really deep moment, I look into your eyes, get close to you in the beautiful silence, and as you're looking at me and my arms wrap around you, I start fingering through my scales behind your back.

We go together like valve oil and valves.

I may like playing with a clarinet even though I play trombone. I may like to play with a violin even though I sing tenor. I might like to play with both a woodwind and a brass instrument even though I play marimba. Or I might even like to play with a saxophone even though I play saxophone too. It's none of your business who I play with. I'm not hurting anybody. But I am adding beautiful music to the world. Maybe you should stop talking, listen, and enjoy?

Is it me or does fortissimo sound like a bad word?

To all the moms that help mend uniforms and hearts, move speakers and mountains, run meetings and homes, all with your boot up our behinds...THANK YOU!

Every time you make a mistake, make sure it's a new one.

Marching band is coming. Can you smell it?
No seriously, do you smell that?

People who don't practice and say they did are my kryptonite.

69

I asked the balloon guy to make me a French horn.
He got visibly uncomfortable and slightly angry.

You know you've reached a special point in your relationship when you're totally lost in your music, you know it, they know it, and then they bail you out with your own personal cue for when you're supposed to come in. Nice.

Percussion I feel ya. I don't like it when people tell me all I do is hit stuff either.

I get nervous holding a string instrument. It seems like it's really easy to set on fire.

Huh, funny. I get the same tingly feeling when I lock in my pitch.

It could be worse. It could be a harmonica band.

Saying homework is optional is like your band director saying, "while we're working over here keep silently fingering through your parts."

If I learned ALL my scales, I wouldn't continue to grow. You don't want that do you?

I find it ironic there is no quiet way to open an instrument case. Just smack the latch and let'r rip. Oh wait, some have zippers. Lucky zipper people.

How about instead of standardized testing we just see if you can stack stands on a stand rack correctly?

If I say I love you, will you let me practice then?

Let me play you my scale. It's the only scale I know, but I will play it the best I can, and it's for you.

I just wrote a symphony...IN MY MIND!

Listen, when you've been in the practice room for hours and a friend comes in and comments on the smell but you don't smell anything...take their word for it and air that puppy out.

The best music groups are the ones who love what they do every day, not just on performance night.

Conductors, if you're going to wear a tux with tails I expect a magic trick or two.

Does the 5 second rule apply to reeds?

I named my instrument my band director's name. It makes for hilarious conversation.

I listen before I look. That way I have the advantage.

When we win a competition let's wear our opponent's mouthpieces around our neck. (Insert primal scream now)

Did you ever notice when you look down at a bassoon
reed it looks like it really wants to kiss you? Well, listen
here, you have to earn this honey.

I'm sorry BAND DIRECTOR. It IS difficult
to have a pencil on my stand every day.

I'm not sure the "music makes you smarter" rule applies
to all sections.

If you think you know the most simply because
you are a senior, then you haven't learned
anything since your were a freshman.

Ending a phrase too early is like sticking your finger in
someone's mouth while they're yawning.

"Why are you doing squats in-between long tones?"
"I'm aiming to hit a double G by spring. Gotta firm
up. Just in case."
"In case what?...oh...ewww."

I know my director works hard, but it's tough to think
about the music sometimes when all you can focus on is
their pit stains.

If music comes from my heart, I wonder
what comes from my other organs?

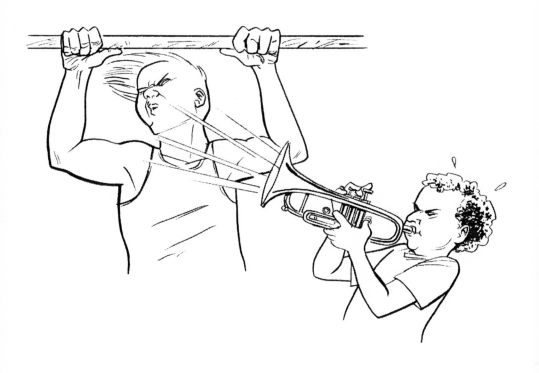

You can do a pull up? I can play a high F.
Consider yourself served.

Sometimes you think you really know your friends and then they go and clap on 1 & 3. It's hard to reply to their text after something like that.

I listen to you like I listen to the band. I hear it, I just think my part is more important at all times.

If band dads were the nuclear fuel of the world, the planet would be glowing and stuff would get done.

Dear people who think music education isn't important....shut up.

You know when someone is staring off while the director is working with a different section like they were zoning out at a camp fire? Then they suddenly realize you were watching them? Then they awkwardly smile at you because you've never really spoken before? Yeah, you're friends now.

I'm so band, I practice Holst's Mars on Valentine's Day.

Saying the instrument seating arrangement doesn't affect the band's sound is like saying it doesn't matter which way the toilet paper roll goes. It does. Over.

New instrument smell > new car smell.

I'd be lying if I said I never thought it would be cool to have some sort of contraption on my wrist that shoots batons out like elvish arrows.

First rule of band is do not talk about band. Unless you're in band, then it's a fact we can't really not talk about it.

You can be like my music. Sometimes I like it, sometimes I don't, but I definitely don't want to stop playing.

Band moms are the best. They take care of us with none of the guilt. Except if you mess up your uniform. Then, LOTS of guilt. Oh man, so much guilt. REALLY REALLY a lot of guilt. I'm sorry. Really sorry.

Sometimes when I'm practicing I pretend I'm working out.

You might judge by IQ, I judge by FF.

If we treated our words with the same love as we treat our music, friends would know less hurt and the world would not know hate.

I thought a polar vortex was the 3 feet of space around an oboe player. Bam.

If I owned my own Magical Mystical Instrument Shop it would include French horns that speak Spanish, clarinets that are actual licorice, and trumpets that don't blow smoke.

The biggest difference between music and math is emotion...and instrument rental fees.

Euphonium players win for most affectionate instrument. They're always hugging it.

Evaluating education based on a test score is like
judging how good a musician a brass player is by
how high they can play.

Mix grandma's feet with stale towel and
month old kale and that's "school horn smell."

I may not be able to afford much but let me play for you
and give you the richest gift I know of.

People don't know what they love, they love what they
know. Which is why music education is so important.

Money can buy you happiness because it
can buy you an instrument...and cookies.

When things are tough, I can't get to the
band room quick enough.

What if there were playing cards for famous musicians
and directors? Pretty sure they wouldn't come packaged
with gum.

Band people don't do stupid stuff. Except for,
you know...that one time...at band camp.

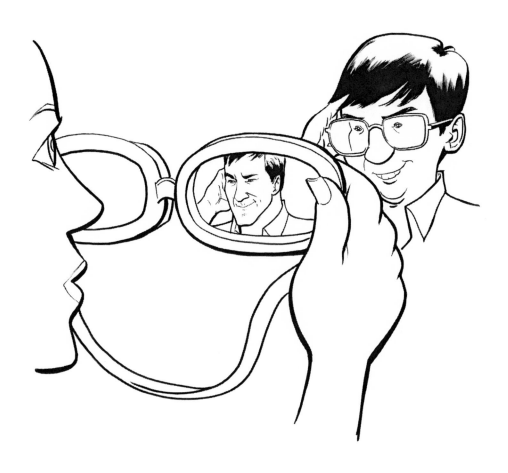

Don't knock my band goggles.
Without them you'd be ugly.

Some people say that music is painted on a canvas of silence.
I like to say music is breaded on the thighs of a Kentucky
Fried Chicken. That's more motivating to me.

A flute player once told me they were an artist not
a musician. Fine. I'm calling you a flartist then.

No. The correct answer is you GET
to come to my band concert.

Music is healthy for both your head and your heart,
just like that special someone...and for some reason
a super chocolate donut cupcake hybrid.

You know when the French horn player gives you
that squinted eye stare? They just decided you are
now their nemesis.

I'm getting a tattoo of a mouthpiece ring on my face.
Then it will never look abnormal.

I didn't miss a note. My instrument simply misspoke.

When I finally play something I never thought I could,
I become stronger than I ever thought I would.

When you walk out of that rehearsal room for the last time, stop, look around, and remember the first time you walked into it. I bet you'll be pretty impressed with the person you've become.

Sometimes you have a rehearsal and you're like whoa.
Sometimes you have a rehearsal and you're like wow.
Sometimes you have a rehearsal and you're like, who farted?
They're all precious memories.

Don't be the jerk who plays everything
perfect but still can't figure it out.

If music is a universal language, band would be the
goofy accented version of it.

You know how when an adult would lick their finger to
clean your face when you were young and it would gross
you out? That's kinda how I feel when the director hands
me a mouthpiece from the extra mouthpiece drawer.

Seriously? We couldn't come up with a
better word than "ictus"?

Playing music is the gift you give to
yourself that others will thank you for.

Great ideas always come during long tones and showers.

If your instrument treated you how you
treat it, would it love you or dent your face?

Sometimes I get my hand jammed up in a brass instrument and walk around pretending I'm bionic.

Not a single music teacher got into music ed. because of the money. Not one. Ironically sometimes it's because they weren't making enough playing, but still you get my point.

Thought I saw a GIF of a director conducting an 8 second slow section. Turns out it was a 7 minute video of a boring director.

An alto sax kinda looks like a goose. Actually, goose butt music sounds pretty good.

Sometimes I get so into my music that it has to remind me we're just friends.

When I tap my fingers on the table like I'm waiting for something, it's usually scale fingerings. Minor if I'm frustrated.

Band peeps always know where the secret bathrooms are.

Is it me, or when you look at a woodwind instrument you feel like you're supposed to find a crayon and try to make your way through the maze?

Sometimes I make music.
Sometimes music makes me.

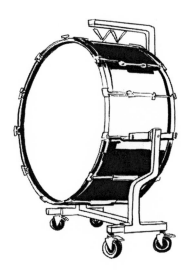

Since I'm having a stressful day give me the biggest mallet you have and get out of the path between me and that bass drum.

We should be able to customize the shape of our
instruments and mouthpieces and etch crests on them like
the knights of old. That way we will be able to tell the evil
players by the spikes and scary insignias.

We all know if you joke about double flat
accidentals, it's out of fear.

When it comes down to it, I'd rather have
my surgeon tell me they played a woodwind
instrument than brass or percussion.

People are better looking when
they make music. Fact.

As long as you're making music you're not
making enemies. Unless you're doing an
experimental piece involving slapping.

Band means different things to different
people. Respect it all.

Marching band is in my blood. I'm FF Positive.

Try asking someone out on a band date.
It's like a regular date only with wonderment.

Sometimes I play air guitar with a clarinet.

Sometimes you have to challenge yourself to grow.
The best things in life are not always in concert B flat.

That moment on the field when you realize the
seat colors in the stands match your uniforms?
Power Up. Sweet.

Sci-fy makes everything cooler. Like the Quantum
Oboe, Interstellar Fusion Trombone, and
Autonomous Galactic Director.

If you get a staff tattoo all down your arm you'll
always have a place to write down that great idea.
That makes sense to me.

When my director is humble, is when I love them the most.

If music is the window to the soul, that makes
practicing glass cleaner. Some of you need to get wipe'n.

In Austraila the toilets flush the other way, the French horns
are in the front, the percussion are model students, and the
trumpets have self-esteem issues. Just what I heard.

Through music I learned to laugh.

Music is only as beautiful as the person
making it...on the inside, I mean.

You and I are hemiola.
Two different feels fitting perfectly in the same measure.
Plus we both know the word hemiola.

Now that I think about it, there really isn't a good
reason to bend your knees dramatically while
playing a concert solo.

Tunekinesis - the power to bend my pitch...
with my mind.

What happens at band camp, stays at band
camp...and the internet.

I still think the treble clef was made up by a young
musician doodling on their standardized test.

Having that moment months or years later when you finally get
what your director was trying to tell you about life, is like when
you realize how triplet rhythms are broken down. Suddenly it's
not so hard. Oh....Ohhhhhh!

Just once, they should have a marching band play in
the Roman Colosseum...without the lions...probably.

"Did you gain weight?"
"No I switched to Eb Clarinet."
"Oh."
"Yeah...jerk."

Much like all the different types of music,
people of all genres are worth listening to.

If you look down the end of an instrument, you can see where dreams come from. Also sometimes bits of potato chips.

I once thought of the perfect melody. Then I forgot it.
Then it was time for cartoons.

> A true friend knows you're forgetful and
> grabs your music for you after you've left.
> Probably borrowed $20 from you as well.

I can circular breathe when I talk.
Try getting a word in now.

> Everyone in band will live on forever. Usually because
> of all the hidden graffiti in the storage room.

Wouldn't it be great if we made a mistake in life we
could just pencil in an accidental marking so we don't
make it again?

> Drum majors get so into the music they want to jump on a
> large downbeat. But within that split second right before,
> they realize they are on a rickety platform so it ends up
> looking like an awkward knee bend. Fierce I tell you.

If I could only find the words to describe
this music...wait what?!

> Band camp is like Disney World. Your family
> yelling at each other, sweating, and can be
> expensive. But everybody loves it.

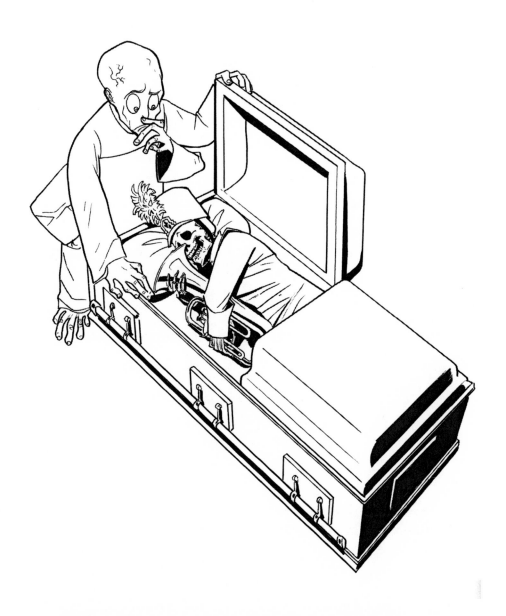

When I die I want to be buried in a cemetery where everyone is buried with their instruments so 1000 years from now when we're dug up by an advanced race they'll go WTF?!

A real leader would rather be down on the field
helping someone struggling with no one watching
than up on the podium in front of thousands.

Having everyone at rehearsal but not mentally
there, is like having full bars but no data.

You don't ever have to say I Love You...while I'm practicing.

Why do instrument lockers sometimes look like animal
cages? Are they afraid we might unleash the beast?

My instrument knows me in ways no person can.
It's awkward at family events.

Music would survive a nuclear apocalypse.
And Twinkies. Not a bad deal.

I can remember that performance any way I want to.
I did not miss that note. Nope, didn't miss it.

You're hilariously musical. Figure that compliment out.

I love you. Now shut up and listen to me play this sonata.

A true friend will count the 57 measures of rest before your solo with you.

Music is a serious business. Ok, I can't even say
that with a straight face. Lighten up.

It's not a gut. It's a perfectly sculpted
warm air machine.

Sometimes I accidentally swear at the end of a really great
performance from all the emotion, and when I get my finger
caught in my instrument case latch, and when you make me
mad, and when I'm telling a great story, and when...

I don't know how to spin a rifle. That doesn't stop me
from picking one up and walking around acting like I do.

OUCH! I touched the cut time!

It's hard to be creative when you're told what,
when, and how to play. Improvise your life.

Sometimes everything comes together.
Sometimes it all falls apart. Just keep playing.

My instrument will never hurt me...well except
that one time...

Music is a great place to go when you don't want to be found.

Trombone players use their slide spray bottles just for a quick drink of water. You know it, I know it. Let's not pretend anymore.

I have climbed the most dangerous peaks. I have sailed oceans in storms that have only existed in legends. I have traveled to the very depths of hell and back but I will never, NEVER again bare the rage-filled gaze of the percussionist watching me pick up a timpani improperly. This I swear.

If I give everything to the music, I won't have anything left for you. Tough choice.

"Digital sheet music" is a director's conspiracy. It's too easy to not forget your music.

When you have a bad performance, do it again, better and wiser, and you'll never be underestimated.

What good are well chiseled abs if they don't do anything? I'd rather be able to play a double G. Ok, that's not true.

Not knowing a math equation is not as bad as not knowing your part. Not because math is less important, but because others are counting on your part.

The more you practice, the longer you live...happily.

Dating someone who knows nothing about music has its advantages...if you suck.

Directors assess who can play oboe by intelligence and creepy long pinky fingers. Makes you want to totally look every time you meet an oboe player now don't it?

Nobody outside of a music group can understand the
true power and impact of a great story from the podium.

What if 5 of us had instruments with special powers
and could combine to form a super robot thing? Like a
nerdy musical Power Rangers team. Well...nerdier.

That awkward moment when your band director missteps up
on the podium and fails completely on a cool recovery.

No no baby. It's not you. It's me...um and
my section leader.

Band heaven is a lot like regular heaven, except the LESS you
practice the better you get. Band hell is nothing like regular
hell. You have to play in sweltering heat, with extremely painful
uniforms, to a crowd that doesn't appreciate you...oh wait...

Plungers for brass instruments are wicked
cool...except if they're used.

A wise, extremely talented euphonium player once
said to me, "Would you like fries with that?"

Drummers, what if I told you the drums are going to
start hitting back? Not so big and bad now are ya?

**Some people just simply can't conduct soft
sections. DO NOT let those people pet your dog.**

We compete to test our skill, but we play to test our hearts.

I want to live in that space between thirds that tingles slightly when perfectly in tune. It's peaceful and I'm sure the rent is cheaper.

When I'm tired of practicing, I'm not really tired of practicing. I'm tired of needing to rest in order to do other things life makes me do.

If the world were a band right now I'd say that everyone thinks they have a solo and no one practiced.

If politics is the only possible reason you think you didn't get the part, you missed an opportunity to get better.

I celebrated my mom today by waking her up to all 12 major scales which I now know because of all her support. This B major scale at 6am is for you Mom.

Olympians listen to music before they go out and make history. I mean I'm sure there is some working out involved but that's just a coincidence.

Life is like music. You're meant to constantly practice because it will never be perfect.

I play loud because the music is so excited to get out of me.

Santa makes his list in score order.

When you connect with someone musically it's like your hearts are touching but without all the mess that would normally be caused by touching two actual hearts together.

Some demand that more money be spent on devices in schools that help enhance a person's learning. I agree, buy more instruments.

I always adjust my instrument when we tune even though I have no idea if I'm sharp or flat. I consider it "band polite."

I threw a football once. Totally threw a bullet spiral back to the ref after it veered off and hit the bass drum. Nailed it.

I'm lost in my music has two meanings, one you'll believe.

Sometimes I don't recognize you right away unless you're sitting at the same angle I see you during rehearsal.

Be a good listener. Did you ever play great music for someone not paying attention?

There IS a difference between playing your instrument and making out with your instrument. Most people just don't care though. Play on, bow chicka wow wow.

**Lots and lots of Pixie Stix are a great way to
prepare for rehearsal.**

Be good to your band. Treat it well. Take
care of it and it will do the same for you.

> Be aware, practicing lip trills without a
> mouthpiece can be uncomfortable for
> those around you.

How come the object we're supposed to watch the most, many
of us from a distance, is a short stick thinner than a pencil?

> The only phrase that provides a sense of
> safety and awkward concern at the same time
> is, "Don't worry I'm a band parent."

Listen, and you might see something you've
never seen before. Weird right?

> If I don't play music for a while I feel like
> I've lost something. Like my keys, I'm
> always leaving them in my case.

Saying something is musical always has a positive
connotation. That's not a coincidence.

> I love you until the end of cut time.

Of course I believe in magic.
I'm a musician.

My music is more than just me and my instrument.
It's more than me being part of my band.
It's the way I choose to connect with the human race,
in a way that we can all understand.

Since you didn't mark it last time, if you miss that
E natural again I'm flicking a booger at you.

"What do you play?"
"Timpani."
"Weird."

It's one thing to be inspired by what you do.
It's another to be inspiring because of it.

If teachers in cartoons sound like trombones,
what do trombone teachers sound like?

For the holidays I FINALLY got an instrument that
is in-tune. Coincidentally it will come in handy with
the extra practice I've recently been doing. Wait...

I will provide life's necessities of water, food,
shelter, love, and music to my child. I will also
teach them how to stick their tongue out, burp
real loud, and our super secret handshake.

It's a bummer when your director yells at you all
the time for forgetting what you just rehearsed.
Good thing you have a bad memory.

You're allowed to love all types of music.
Same rule applies to people.

**I'm pretty sure if I had a cat, it would play oboe.
Cats just seem kinda oboe-ish ya know?**

No need to mic the woodwinds. If they were meant to
be that loud they'd be built with more chutzpah.

Ever play so loud you rattle your skull?
Some people drink coffee. I do that.

It's weird if your dream vacation get-a-way is a
band trip. Don't let anyone tell you differently.

After years of marching band I'm sure I can
be that awesome waiter who carries 12 trays
at once. Roll heel toe!

Practicing even after everyone else says it
sounds fine...

Please wash your feet and your
mouthpiece. Everyday I'm going
to make you a little less gross.

Dear next greatest science fiction movie maker, please include
an interpretation of marching bands in the future. I would like
to see my vision of instruments made from liquid metal that
change shape at the will of the player come to fruition. Also at
least one cyborg evil judge to add to the drama.

If I win the lottery, I'm buying every band
kid their own instrument.

I hold my utensils like drumsticks traditional grip
while waiting for my food. Pretty sure people can tell
I'm not a drummer.

I may or may not have held my instrument
inappropriately a few times because I thought I was
being funny. Don't judge me, you've done it too liar.

Courage can be knowing you're not the best player in
the room but still offering your musical thoughts.

When you walk out after an amazing rehearsal,
for that moment...you're invincible.

If woodwinds can make their own
reeds then I want a smelting class.

If you're serious about music, then you'll allow
yourself to laugh when you feel you don't deserve it.

Band can make you grow up or throw up.
Either way it's your choice.

If instruments were animals I'm pretty sure
percussionists would be wild boar.

No my belly's this big because I've been practicing my
breathing so much. Pure muscle...and a few nachos.

I missed my entrance because I was
just so into the music.

My instrument judges me.

And for my next trick I will blow air through an oddly shaped piece of metal or wood and create complex mathematical waveforms that make tiny bones in your head vibrate to trigger a sense of joy and pleasure. But the real magic will be if I can get paid for it.

I wonder which is harder to put on, brake pads or clarinet pads.

It's not that percussionists aren't affectionate or that it's difficult to hug with a harness on. It's more like...how do I put this...they hate you.

I live for Fortissimo, but secretly yearn for Pianissimo. Like a professional wrestler.

I have a favorite accent. It's a "French Staccato." It's like a regular staccato, but I have way nicer shoes.

Classical Alto Saxes are like Vampires. They suck the fun out of you and then you become one. Naw, I'm just kidding. But seriously...

When there's no end in sight, stop looking and start listening.

Why is the director always pointing? So rude.

**No your heart didn't skip a beat. I just live in 5/8.
Won't you join me?**

Is it too much to ask for a coffee maker in the instrument locker room? I'm no diva, but what is this the middle ages? Oh, and please be sure to rinse it out when I'm done. Sheesh.

It's ok if you'd rather be playing in the graduation orchestra than waiting to get your diploma. That doesn't mean you won't run like hell when it's over.

I count rest measures on my fingers. Sometimes my section does it all together. On occasion we're still late...but we're late together and isn't that what really counts?

I care about the environment so I bought a hybrid instrument. Runs on part air and part awesomeness.

If I were a fish I would be a musical fish.

When your director conducts so hard their cheeks shake, think about it in slow mo.

Music is only as beautiful as the person making it...on the inside, I mean.

Sometimes I misjudge how close my mouthpiece is to my face.

Inspiration comes in all forms. Including freshmen.

**I'm pretty sure someone in band somewhere is
a superhero.**

I'm going to use the word "epic" to describe every piece of
music I talk to my friends about and see if they notice.

When I feel bad I put on sad music.
It's just one of those things.

There are some double standards I'm ok with. Bands
getting stadium practice time but football teams not
getting band room workout time is all good with me.

Only analyze chord progressions of pop tunes
playing on the radio with other music people.
It's for your own good. The world isn't ready
for that quite yet...soon though.

I like practicing with you because you understand
the positivity and purpose in my mistakes.

Is it ironic that the tests designed to rate
and rank our intelligence are dumb? Wait,
what's the definition of irony again?

In the future when we all have one robot
arm I'm gonna play some mad scales.

Are you involved with music to escape who
you really are or to be who you really are?

Reading in different keys and somehow saying
the same thing. Music is simply amazing.

If I had telekenesis I would join winter guard
and do the most amazing tricks.
Probably do other stuff too.

We are not the lower band, we are another band. And
we play with just as much love for what we do as you.

The people who study apes are the only ones who
understand how it feels when someone calls a
Euphonium a baby tuba. It's not a monkey!

There's a line between practicing too much and making out
with your instrument. A very thin blurry line.

I want to live until 100.
I've got too much music to listen to.

I've only cried in three places.
Where I was born, your arms, and the band room.

It isn't the band directors that act like they're
perfect that influence the most. It's the ones
that act like they're not.

I want to secretly replace the baton with a slightly
curved one and see if the band plays any smoother.

When music becomes a business, it ceases to be art.
When schools become a business, it ceases to be education.
No wonder we struggle to value music education.

**Drum Majors should enter the field on unicorns
'cause on the field, anything's possible.**

A section leader who thinks they're the best is like decaf coffee. Ineffective.

It's possible to look cool walking in slow-mo with an instrument. I just have to figure out how.

The only reason I cry is to sample the sound my tear makes when it hits the floor. Then I remix that bad boy.

After an amazing performance of a piece, we should bang our chests and clank helmets. Oh, we should start wearing helmets.

Sometimes I get so into my music that I close my eyes and move my head passionately. Then I go sharp and crack a note.

If I had 4 hands, I would totally play a trombone/guitar duet with myself. If I had 4 hands.

If we standardized all the music, it wouldn't be very good music. If we standardized all the tests, they wouldn't be very good tests. Oh, wait...

When you're the only one who laughs at your director's joke, don't be startled by the weird looks coming your way...that's normal.

We perform surgery with lasers, send information through thin air, and can create whole worlds with a single computer. Conductors still use a stick.

Playing your last show ever is just as bitter sweet as raising a
tiger from birth only to have to let it go. You want to keep it,
but you know if you do it will one day maul your face off.

Chair placement doesn't mean much
when everyone has to march in step.

Politics brings out the worst in us.
Marching Band brings out the best of us.
Less Politics. More Marching Band.

If we had to raise our instruments from birth we
would all be amazing musicians. You know, cause
we wouldn't want to hurt baby instruments.

I want a world where we can upgrade our
instruments like in video games. I would add Bell
Fire Charm and Valves of Power.

If a gifted musician teaches private
lessons, is it considered regifting?

It feels more like I'm coming home for the day
when I walk into the band room in the morning
than when I walk into my house at night.

When people tell me I can start over with
a blank page, mine is staff paper.

All's I'm say'n is there is a large business
opportunity investing in bus ventilation systems
for marching bands.

If more people had music in their education, there
would be more available sticks and less clenching.

Talking to you is just as frustrating as trying
to write note heads at the perfect angle. My
computer will solve both problems.

Listen here music. It's called a staff.
So get to work and make me some money

I love you so much that I'll let you listen to me practice.

What if you got your math grade by auditions? Like you'd
have to come in front of a panel of judges solve your best
math equations, fill out all addition, subtraction, division,
and multiplication tables, and then sight solve an age
appropriate worksheet. Still doesn't seem fair.

Your director works out so much they look like
a buff oompa loompa T-Rex waving their arms.
It's hard to play soft and sweetly watching that.

I invented a new fragrance. It's a mix of inside old back-up
instrument case and audition anxiety. It's pretty potent.

Music is my life. Or is it my life is my music?
I'm just gonna go practice and let it figure itself out.

When life gets you by your roots, try a different inversion.

If we all had rocket boots we could do drill in 3D.

Great musical groups don't hope they'll get
better, they believe they will.

What? I'm a brass player in orchestra. I don't play for
like 643 measures and I had to go to the bathroom.

If someone says music isn't powerful, they've obviously never
met Brett, the 6 foot 3 all-state wrestler/bass clarinet player...
or Jen, the 5 foot 2 sax player who can destroy you emotionally
in a 10 second conversation. Music isn't powerful? I have the
battle scars to show it....punk.

I once yelled hello down my bell. Yesterday
someone yelled back. That was weird.

Asking if music people are smart is like asking
if Yoda's boogers are green. Well, I mean...
you're in music, you get my point.

The silence from everyone in the group after
you realize you played something special is
often just as beautiful.

I think it's cool when string player's bows shred as they
get intense. My lacquer does that sometimes.

My third valve finger seems like no matter how hard I
practice, it will always be the last kid picked for kickball.

**Turns out my instrument IS a Transformer.
But it just turns into another instrument.**

You can love your instrument, just don't be IN love with your instrument. It makes for socially awkward situations and I won't be able to take you anywhere.

There's no better feeling than picking your instrument back up after not playing for a long time. Wait, yes there is...not sounding terrible.

Practice ripping your instrument off your face as much as you do scales in thirds. You gotta look good ya know?

If you put two instrument bells together it's like they're kissing, but just as good friends. We're an affectionate people.

(deep breath) There's nothing worse than waiting through the unspoken hidden silence of the slight movement in your director's face after you completely blow a significant part in a piece you're performing because you didn't practice the way you said you did, you know it, the director knows it, and there's still five and a half minutes left.

If my instrument was made out of chocolate, I would have a serious conflict of interest.

Normal people can't appreciate a whole note being played at a calming mezzo piano with a tender soft tongued beginning, released by the perfectly timed stoppage of air. Don't be normal.

Sometimes my mind wanders while I play. It's when I do my best thinking.

Watching someone experience their first drum corps show can make you a little bit nervous as you wonder who's gonna clean up after they soil themselves.

I remember the first time a director asked me
to sing my part. The reaction was like asking a
lawyer to build a piece of furniture.

There's nothing like the calmness of being the only one
in the band room in-between the end of the school day
and the evening performance. It's my zen place.

Air Euphonium and Air Oboe don't have the same ring as
Air Guitar. See, they DO have something in common.

It was once said a jazz piano player went
crazy trying to swing whole notes.

If I could keep a marching band in my pocket I
would. It would be weird when it played though.
"I'm not happy to see you...just my march'n band."

Low brass embouchures always look like
they're holding back a belch. Then they play...
coincidence?

Try whispering "forte" to yourself a couple times.
Weird right? Now look around at the people
staring at you. Weird right?

Yes, I admit it. I conduct the pop music on the
radio. Too bad I sometimes can't give a cut off.

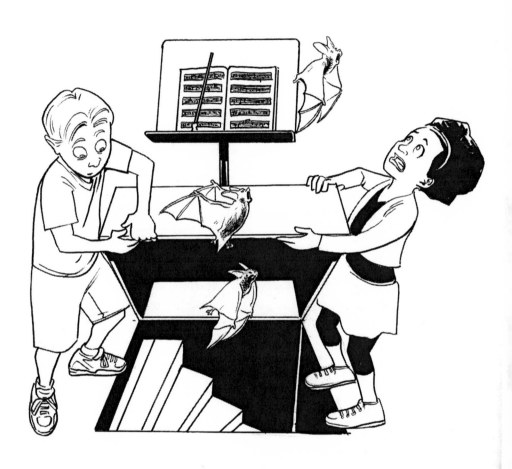

**Underneath the podium is a stairwell.
I just know it.**

Ok make up your mind. You either want no talking at all,
or you want me to help my section get better. But you can't
have your cake and eat it too...wait you have cake?

Sometimes your band director tells the perfect story
at the perfect time and powerful things happen.

If you had a tuba and oboe player switch instruments and asked
them to play double quadruple f, I'm pretty sure the oboe would
blow up. The instrument, not the player. Although...

Am I the only one that has dreamt about saving the
day during a bank robbery using my instrument?

Why all the blah blah and yak yak yak?
Can't we all just play together?

If aliens came and visited our planet which
would you rather have them meet, the band
or the football team? Just say'n.

Went to the gym today and bench pressed like two
tubas yo. And not those wussy tiny F tubas either.
I was all Bb horns baby.

Funny how the only ones who ask to prove the
link between music education and higher level
thinking are the ones who had none.

**It finally happened.
You played so loud...you pooped yourself.
Not easy to do on Marimba.**

When you break up with someone I recommend an English
horn playing a soft melody in the background while you
do it. It eases the tension by taking their mind off of being
dumped and onto "Is that an English horn? What the..."

Does one wrong note ruin the melody or
create something more interesting?

You meet someone and you're like whoa they're totally
awesome, I'm in love. Then they pick up an instrument and
kill it, then you're like whoa they're outta my league. Then you
practice harder for the wrong reason, but you're ok with that.

I'm just saying if they want us to sit at the front of the
chair maybe they shouldn't make the seats so big?

My love for you is unconditional.*

You know when you have eye crust first thing in
the morning? Sometimes I feel my instrument
has the same thing when I first take it out.

Please don't tell me you have perfect pitch,
it's like telling me not to hit the red button.

When the competition seems too big for your
little band remember the competition exists
because of you. Not so big now huh?

*Does not include holding, trying, or
breathing on my brand new instrument.

141

**Sometimes people say they know more than me.
That's ok, I can play my instrument on a unicycle.
Plus their momma's ugly.**

Owning a bassoon is like owning a pool cue. You don't
really tell anyone about it, but when it's the right time,
you're a badass when you take it out.

You may not notice the Euphonium, but you
can feel when they're not there. Same goes
for when they're playing.

I went to the scariest haunted house tonight. It was
actually a regular house but no one was involved with
music. Ahhh!!

The real competition is to see how much you can eat
from concessions to the stands. Challenge accepted.

You might live in a world where music isn't
important, but it's the wrong one.

When you rock that duet section where you're playing
with someone across the band is like when two
different parts of the world find common ground and
something wonderful happens.

Your director may yell at you to clap on 2 & 4, but we all know
what they're like in the club.

Sometimes I place my stand at 45 inches high
at 86° so the director can't see me put my
head in my hands & close my eyes.

I'm not tapping my foot loudly, it just fell asleep during
rehearsal. What's your excuse?

Directors should conduct more with their eyebrows, except if they have a unibrow. Then please don't do that.

The only thing leadership has to do with you is whether or not you realize leadership is about everyone else but you.

Playing bass as a second instrument automatically makes your first instrument cooler.

This one time, at band camp... I rocked the crap out of my part, had a killer sectional, perfected our show, and got a standing ovation during our first performance. Put that in your joke and smoke it. (Don't smoke)

You can't have harmony without two notes. Funny how the same is true for dissonance.

The same urge that makes me straighten paper clips occurs when I look at a treble clef.

Music people dirty jokes tend to be dirtier than normies' dirty jokes. Ironically it's because we're more mature. Diarrhea.

Imagine if we were rewarded monetarily by the number of lessons we learned. Pretty sure music teachers would be the most valued occupation in the world.

No I didn't get in a fight. I just get really excited when I salute.

If they can make a crazy straw why can't they make a crazy flute...oh, wait.

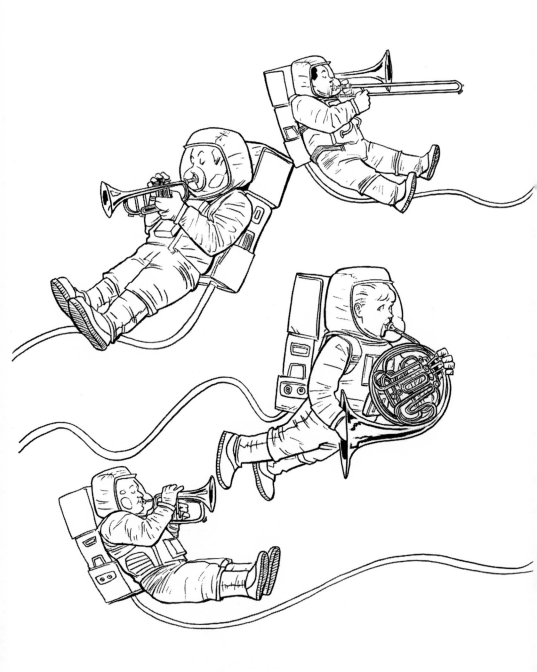

**If I play my instrument in space
will I move backwards?**

Band is hilarious. I'm serious about that.

"That sounded better in my head."
"Then we know what the problem is don't we?"

Sometimes my mind wanders to something
inappropriate during the slow serious parts...but
that somehow makes it appropriate.

Give the gift of music. Better throw in a
card too or else they'll think you're cheap.

"Hitting something musically is beautiful," says the
percussionist. So the next time you punch someone
in the forehead be sure to do it with musical integrity.
Then yell, "How do you like my art?"

It's the absolute best when you need a little
inspiration and your band director comes through.

Sometimes I sit down at the piano and start playing then
realize I don't know how to play. But I don't stop.

I will always be there for you, unless I have rehearsal.

You know that moment when the waves of two notes
coming closer and closer in tune suddenly stop, and all
you hear is one calming pitch? Yeah, you're that.

If I go to a comic convention will my band nerdiness and comic nerdiness cancel each other out like two wave forms matching opposite amplitudes?

On days I feel ordinary, music makes me feel special.

Someone once told me music heals all
wounds. That person obviously hasn't
had their hand caught in their slide.

I play so aggressively when I'm hungry.

The irony is if we cut music programs to pay for more
math and science we end up with less scientists and
engineers. Well, good ones anyway.

Imagine if we got paid to dream instead of
encouraged to forget them.

When you make fun of someone because of your
own insecurities it's like when your director
is lost in the score and stops the group only to
criticize "something they heard."

I still think we should combine science and
music into one superclass. Imagine the evil
genius that could come from that.

Sometimes I practice really angry and play
the snot out of that sweet, soft melody.

We don't need weapons, I can
blow you away with my music.

149

**A toast to the notes that only use one hand to play.
You allow me to scratch when I really need to.**

Playing barefoot just makes you more
"artsy" ya know?

Sometimes I just go crazy with my
instrument and play whatever random
noise comes to mind just to be silly.

Imagining the world without music is like having to
eat raw brussel sprouts while doing calculus in a beige
room after you just stubbed your toe. It sucks.

It's pretty hard to create music and not feel
like you're moving forward in some small way.

"Tell me you love me?"
"I can't. It's beyond words. I can only
  describe it by playing for you."
"Better practice then."

Secretly rehearse a piece you're going to
play later in the year. Then after the group
reads it for the first time ask your director
if they have anything challenging.

Music people come in all different sizes,
but our hearts are always large.

The best thing about practicing is being proud of YOURSELF.

I wish my school horn case had more secret hidden compartments where I might find a magical trinket from bands past.

I will fight for music! I mean, not like a real fight-fight.
I'm more of a fight with my ideals classical musician
type soooooo, I've never actually been in a fight. Saw
one once though. No, no, that's a lie too.

Music is a medicine no pharmaceutical
company can profit from. Unfortunately
neither can musicians.

The room where music is taught needs to
be the safest place for everyone.

What if instead of giving someone the middle
finger you played an F concert exercise?
Seems less confrontational.

The band doesn't play music for the football team.
The football team plays football for the band.

Next time my director is just freaking out on the
podium, I'm going to simply get up without saying
a word and place a cupcake on their stand.

Others can help you sound amazing.
But only you can make yourself a musician.

I am a doubled up 6th chair player. I will rock
the snot out of my parts and you will love what
the 6th chair doubled up player has to offer.
Then we will all go for pancakes.

153

If people can look like their pets, can they look like their instruments?

When I get in an argument, and I mean a really big
argument, sometimes I'll take out my horn and play
something really loud then rip it off my face just to
emphasize my point.

Of course my test scores are higher because I
do music, you don't get multiple choice in an
audition. You learn you gotta come to play baby.

Having a nose ring while playing the tuba has got
to be the brass equivalent of a sizzle cymbal.

Band drama is more dramatic than regular drama.
It has a soundtrack.

Not good at emotional facial expressions while
playing? Then just let the music do the talking.
Don't let your face screw it up.

Just when you think you sound awesome,
you burp up Mountain Dew.

The door to the band room being locked when you really
need some "band room time" is like when you wake up on
Christmas and there is an electrified booby-trapped 9 foot
fence surrounding your presents.

Sometimes I don't like the music we're
playing in band. Then I get a solo and
it's suddenly not so bad.

I've worked so hard on lip trills I can now bench press with my face.

If you marry me, you marry the band. Except
the tubas. You don't have to marry the tubas.
I wouldn't wish that on anyone.

Is it me or do oboes look like tribal weapons that
blow poison darts? Note to self, be nice to oboes.

I once met a flute player who could blow out one
candle surrounded by ten others. She was like
an airflow sniper. Too bad she couldn't be that
careful with my heart (...tear).

Sometimes I think high notes are scary,
but then realize your face is.

If I'm crying it's only because someone scratched
my instrument. NO OTHER REASON!

Woodwinds use a delicate screwdriver to
fix their instruments. Brass use a hammer.
That's a metaphor if I ever heard one.

Let's build a time machine and go back. You can't
change your instrument, but you CAN change your
hairstyle. In fact...I insist.

I'm just say'n, baritones are traditionally
known for not being great colorers growing
up. They tend to eat the crayons.

157

I wish I had a professionally built practice room at home. Not to practice, just for the quiet. Life is loud.

Never pack a metronome in your carry-on luggage
without pulling the batteries out first. Bad scene.

Sometimes I try to balance my music stand perfectly
in the center instead of tightening the screw at the
bottom. It keeps me occupied during rests.

I hope I'm half the man my band director was.
Band Directors don't have time to work out that much.

I wish I could be a conductor while walking around.
I'd give so many people cut offs and never cue them
back in. Except for you...you can come back in.

Love the epic breakdowns in rehearsal where you have no
idea what happened, who started where, and everyone just
laughs and starts over.

I like practicing with you because you understand
the positivity and purpose in my mistakes.

I know I come off all big and bad, but secretly, between
you and me, I sometimes wish I sat in the front row.

If I have to sing my part in rehearsal to get better, then I think
it's only fair the singers learn to play their parts to not suck.

Do you have to be really smart to play the oboe?
Or does playing the oboe make you really smart?
Seriously, what the heck?

I blare wind ensemble music out of my car while driving with my sunglasses on and top down just to prove I'm better than you.

The benefit of being in the back during rehearsal is that
each day you can scan everyone in the group consistently
reevaluating who you would or would not date.

Staying in the practice room when you don't feel
like playing is like being in an empty relationship.

I love when I listen to a piece of music and
smile because of the memory it brings up.

They might be able to make a computer sound
like a real musician, but they'll never be able
to make it smell like one.

Your talent may get you there, but your
choices will keep you there.

If everyone stepped on the gas at the same time
there would be no traffic. Similar to if everyone
believed in music education at the same time except
instead of traffic it would be war, poverty, and hate.

For anyone who has lived with music
knows the baton is really a magic wand.

Music helps you be courageous. That's why
you listen to it during the bad times.

Dance and art get you the visuals, literature the specifics,
and music the soul. Everything else gets you grades.

To the person that designs concert white dress shirts…you're not helping.

When you find someone older or younger than
you that had your same director it's like you're
suddenly from the same bloodline.

Sometimes you may need to use your personal
mute. Not because people don't want to hear you,
but maybe they just need to hear you a little less.

If every band and orchestra had each member write a
poem, collect and bind them in a book to be placed in a
library with others from all over the world, it very well
might be the most beautiful and insightful place on earth.

Clean your instrument out often otherwise
people will think you fart when you play.
Percussion you have no excuses. You did it.

I'm going to build Band World. It's just like Disney World
full of enjoyment and wonder, it just won't make any money.

Going through your first chair placement
challenge is like your band bar mitzvah.

When you find out someone plays the same
instrument as you, it's kinda like meeting an actor
that plays a relatable character and assuming they
understand your life...except they do.

When I lose something I fill the space with music
and suddenly it doesn't seem lost at all.

Leave it all on the field. Except your clothes.
Please take your clothes with you.

Your director isn't perfect. Nor should they be. That's
the selflessness of teaching. They give you their
wisdom and mistakes.

                    I think directors pick their noses with their batons.
                    No other reason to bang the stand that hard.

The farther apart we are the more phasing affects
our relationship. Let's have a common point to
focus on and we'll get in sync.

                    When you catch a look with someone else in
                    the group while performing and smile with
                    your eyes it's like an unspoken musical hug.

My instrument locker is like my inbox without a
search feature. If it's not on the top, it's gone forever.

                    If you always listen to people who tell you
                    to play it differently, than you're always an
                    artist who only creates someone else's art.

I still remember the time I opened my first instrument
case. My eyes widened, my mouth watered, and I
couldn't help but think, "What the hell is that smell?"

                    I admit sometimes I play on the percussion
                    equipment knowing it makes them mad.

"Honestly, I practice in the bathroom for the acoustics,"
"You play piano."

Whoever can play the highest note can marry me.
BUT, it has to be with great tone. Otherwise no deal.

I've always heard a music person will end up
curing a serious disease. I believe that cure will
be found growing in a tuning slide somewhere.

I choose to listen. You should too.

The reason trombone players sometimes wear
velcro shoes is because their spit valve gets
caught in their laces. Not because they don't
know how to tie a shoe...ok, it's a little of both.

Sometimes I write something and think it is the dumbest
thing I ever wrote. Then I play it again the next day and it's
genius. Then one more time...it's dumb again.

You know how to be able to play your
instrument faster? Flame decals.

I'm pretty sure French horns were designed by the same
person who created the Chinese finger traps. I may or may
not have a horn attached to my wrist right now.

Brass players, a pelvic thrust does not
make you player higher or louder.
String players...it might.

I've finally identified the "school horn" smell.
It's either the trapped souls of lost alternates or
forgotten sour cream & onion pretzels.

Hey where did you're creepy long
fingernails go? Nice new reeds though,
didn't know they came in packs of ten.

> I'm sorry. I know I'm a brass player, but the Marimba
> just looks so fun. It's like when you were four and that
> cool aunt got you the seven key xylophone in multiple
> colors. Way more awesome than the weird uncle
> getting you that fake transformer "change-o-bot" thing.

Write a love song for someone and watch them fall head
over heels for you. Just don't play it on your instrument.
Doesn't seem to have the same effect on a bass clarinet.

> If something accidentally flies out of your director's
> mouth and onto your leg during a concert, don't panic.
> Think happy thoughts and hope it doesn't start to smell.

If celebrities started wearing sousaphones as an
accessory, would you wear one? I would, except
that was SO last year.

> Ok, when you have to "dance" while playing,
> move your whole body. Just don't bend at
> your waist and wiggle around, you look weird.
> Like awkward cousin weird.

At first I think it's gross when my instrument tastes
like potato chips...but then I crave potato chips.

If you grow a beard keep it under control. No one needs to wonder where the mouthpiece goes.

If you put different accent and dynamic markings over
the words "I love you" each time you say it, it makes it
more tolerable. Try staccato I love you. Much more fun.

Great tone starts with great air, oh and
removing all cleaning tools and supplies
from within the instrument.

Sometimes during really long rests, I play
imaginary connect the dots with the dirty spots on
my instrument to pass the time.

I need someone more stable, not some
wobbly music stand I can't trust during a
solo. Know what I mean?

I have seen the boogie man. He's in the hat box room.
He gets free rent during concert band season.

The day before the big concert, everyone dye your
hair various shades of purple. The band will look like
a giant bruise and you can call it performance art.

The best way to get someone to listen to
your music, is to listen to theirs.

Music is about inclusion.
If yours isn't, it's not music you're making.

**We have a choice of what we teach our children.
Choose wisely.**

Believe

Peace with a whole lotta hair grease. See ya.

- The 13th Chair

Special Thank You

Jessica
Grae
Scott
Mom
Meg
Ken Martinson
Scott McCormick
Music For All

The
13th
Chair

www.the13thchair.com

CPSIA information can be obtained at www.ICGtesting.com
Printed in the USA
LVOW07s1212301015

460440LV00001B/1/P